The Royal Ballet
AT COVENT GARDEN

1. *Cinderella*. Frederick Ashton

2. *Giselle*. Antoinette Sibley and Anthony Dowell

The Royal Ballet

AT COVENT GARDEN

Text by DAVID VAUGHAN

Photographs by LESLIE E. SPATT
and JENNIE WALTON
with Edward Griffiths, Mike Humphrey
and Rosemary Winckley

DANCE BOOKS LTD
9 Cecil Court London WC2N 4EZ

First published in 1975
by Dance Books Ltd
9 Cecil Court London WC2
Printed in Great Britain
by BAS Printers Limited
Wallop Hampshire

Designed by Peter L. Moldon

ISBN 0 903102 17 X (cloth)
ISBN 0 903102 18 8 (paper)

Photographs
Leslie E. Spatt: 2, 5, 6, 12, 16, 18, 19, 21, 22, 24–26, 32, 33, 34, 37–39, 43, 44, 51, 53, 55, 59, 63, 72, 77, 79–82, 85, 89, 94, 100, 102, 105, 107–109, 111–114, 116, 119, 121, 125, 126, 130, 135, 139–146, 151. Also front cover photograph of Antoinette Sibley and Anthony Dowell in *The Sleeping Beauty* and back cover photograph of Merle Park and David Wall in *The Walk to the Paradise Garden*
Jennie Walton: 1, 3, 7, 13, 14, 20, 27, 29–31, 35, 36, 41, 42, 48–50, 52, 56, 58, 60, 62, 65–67, 69, 70, 74, 76, 78, 83, 84, 87, 95–99, 101, 103, 104, 118, 120, 122, 124, 127–129, 131, 133, 136–138, 149, 150, 152–154
Edward Griffiths: 8, 10, 11, 15, 17, 73, 75, 106
Mike Humphrey: 23, 28, 45, 46, 54, 57, 68, 71, 86, 90–93, 110, 123, 132, 134, 148
Rosemary Winckley: 4, 9, 40, 47, 61, 64, 88, 115, 117, 147

The Royal Ballet: past, present and future

"And I dare affirm if we had half the Encouragement in England, that they have in other Countries, you might in a short time have as good Dancers in England as they have in France. . . ."

Henry Purcell
Preface to *The Fairy Queen*

When Ninette de Valois opened a school in London in 1926 with the grandiose title of the Academy of Choreographic Art, we may assume that she visualized the time, five years later, when she and a group of her dancers would start giving performances at a theatre—two theatres, as it turned out—to which they were attached as a resident company. The Old Vic near Waterloo Station, an old theatre, and Sadler's Wells in Islington, a new one, had permanent drama and opera companies that shuttled back and forth between the two theatres. At first the dancers' function was to perform incidental dances in plays and operas but it was not long before regular evenings of ballet began to be given as well. It would not be surprising to learn that de Valois even looked forward twenty years to the occasion when her company reopened the Royal Opera House, Covent Garden, after the war, with the great production of the Petipa-Tchaikovsky classic *The Sleeping Beauty*, and to their conquest of America with the same ballet in 1949. One of de Valois's greatest gifts was this ability to look ahead, the recognition that any action she took would have its consequences ten, twenty, thirty years later.

The company's wartime tours of the provinces, alternating with London seasons at the New (now the Albery) Theatre made the Vic-Wells, later Sadler's Wells, Ballet Britain's National Ballet in everything but name, and official recognition of this fact finally came in 1956 when a royal charter of incorporation signed by Queen Elizabeth II gave the title of Royal Ballet to the main company, its touring section, and the school. The inclusion of the last must particularly have gratified Dame Ninette, as she was by then, because having started with a school, she has always realised that without one there can be no company.

The relationship between school and company is reciprocal: the school provides the dancers and the company the teachers who perpetuate the style that has been established through the repertory. In this respect too de Valois pursued a far-sighted policy from the beginning, insisting on the importance of the nineteenth century classics that are the ballet dancer's patrimony: *Giselle*, *Coppélia*, *Swan Lake*, *The Nutcracker*, and *The Sleeping Beauty* were all in the Wells' repertory by the end of the thirties in versions that, though small in scale, were as authentic as possible. Each country in which ballet has taken root has developed a national style through the modification of classic academic technique by the admixture of indigenous characteristics (both of physique and personality) and, equally important, by the discoveries of a great choreographer (not always himself a native of that country)—for example, the Frenchman Marius Petipa in Russia, the Franco-Danish, Auguste Bournonville, in Denmark, and the Russian, George Balanchine, in the United States.

De Valois's own tendency as a choreographer was towards dance drama, and while such works as *Job* and *The Rake's Progress* were important in utilizing native literary and pictorial sources, she realised that she needed to choose as an associate a choreographer whose tendency was more towards pure dance, whose works would thus provide not only a necessary balance in the repertory but also begin to form a native classic style on the basis of the *danse d'école* as embodied in the works of Marius Petipa and the other great choreographers of the nineteenth century.

She decided to put her faith in Frederick Ashton, who though British by birth had been brought up in Peru, a circumstance that gave some of his early work an exotic flavour. He was moreover often accused of being frivolously modish—the truth was that he was very little interested in stories, and at that time "seriousness" was usually judged in terms of subject-matter rather than dance content. (There were a few honourable exceptions among the critics, notably Arnold Haskell.) Dancers, from great established artists like Karsavina and Lopokova to beginners like Pearl Argyle and Maude Lloyd who came, as Ashton did, out of Marie Rambert's studio, always appreciated him because he always discovered their most personal qualities and revealed them to the best advantage. On a pragmatic level, de Valois recognised that Ashton was above all a "pro" whose experience in choreographing not only ballets but musicals, films, anything that came to hand, meant that he could be relied upon to produce two or three well-made works every season that would both show off and extend the dancers' talents. De Valois had already the great good fortune to have enlisted from the beginning the aid of Constant Lambert as musical director of her company—and he was far more than a conductor, a man of enormous literary and artistic cultivation, and a great wit, whose collaboration, she must have known, would be invaluable to Ashton whose instincts in such matters were sound but who still needed guidance.

Joining the company on a permanent basis in 1935, Ashton repaid de Valois's faith in him with a series of works that showed a growing depth and mastery of his medium: *Le Baiser de la fée*, *Apparitions*, *Nocturne*, *Horoscope*, *Dante Sonata*, *The Wanderer*, and, no less important, lighter works like *Les Patineurs* and *A Wedding Bouquet* that have in fact outlived the other. (*Les Rendezvous*, another perennial favourite and a ballet of seminal importance in Ashton's career, dates back to 1933.) It was with an Ashton ballet, *Symphonic Variations*, that the company truly took possession of the Covent Garden stage—for the first performances there of *The Sleeping Beauty* were fairly tentative—and this ballet too was Ashton's purest statement of classicism to date and has been a signature work of the company ever since.

Another important step that the move to the Opera House made possible, indeed inevitable, was the production of new full-length ballets that could take their place beside the classics of the past—Ashton's *Cinderella, Sylvia, Ondine, La Fille mal gardée* (the most English of all ballets), and its pendant work *The Two Pigeons*. Each of these, and shorter Ashton works like *Scènes de ballet, Daphnis and Chloë, Birthday Offering*, and *The Dream*, seems to have crystallized some stage in the company's development; equally important milestones in this history have been the visits to America over the last twenty-five years, which turned the company from a national into an international one, and Margot Fonteyn into its prima ballerina assoluta. With Fonteyn as exemplar the dancers added legibility on a grand scale to their native lyricism, precision, and good manners, absorbing the influence of the more magniloquent Soviet style, first introduced to them by the *émigré* Moscow ballerina Violetta (Prokhorova) Elvin, then massively revealed at the first London season of the Bolshoi in 1956, finally and decisively manifested with the advent of Nureyev in 1962.

As the dancers grew in authority it became important for them to measure themselves not only against the classic rôles of the nineteenth century but against the masterpieces of the twentieth: Diaghilev ballets like Massine's *La Boutique fantasque, The Three Cornered Hat*, and *The Good Humoured Ladies*, Fokine's *Firebird* and *Petrouchka* (his *Les Sylphides* and *Carnaval* were revived at a much earlier date in the company's history), Nijinska's *Les Biches* and *Les Noces*, Balanchine's *Apollo* and *The Prodigal Son* were all added to the repertory over the years, as well as works from the contemporary international repertory like Balanchine's *Agon, Serenade*, and *The Four Temperaments*, Antony Tudor's *Lilac Garden*, and Jerome Robbin's *Dances at a Gathering, Afternoon of a Faun*, and *In the Night*. There have also been creations by outside choreographers—some would say too few of these—notably Tudor's *Shadowplay* and *Knight Errant*, Glen Tetley's *Field Figures* and *Laborintus*, and Rudi van Dantzig's *Ropes of Time*.

Under de Valois the company added to its overseas conquests Leningrad and Moscow, at least equal in importance to New York; when she retired from the directorship in 1963 —the least inactive retirement imaginable—the natural successor was Ashton, who had been officially co-director for some years, and he was followed in 1970 by Kenneth MacMillan, the first choreographer of any importance to have emerged from within the ranks of the company (John Cranko had made his first ballets in South Africa before coming to Britain to join the company—and of course his most important achievements took place elsewhere). MacMillan had already given the company a full-length *Romeo and Juliet* to Prokofiev's score that has by now assumed war-horse status, along with several shorter pieces, notably *The Invitation* and *The Rite of Spring*, that displayed the talents of younger dancers like Lynn Seymour and Monica Mason. He then served a further apprenticeship as director of the ballet in Berlin during which time he made two ballets that have become staples of the home repertory, *Song of the Earth* and *Concerto*.

If the history of a ballet company is in its choreographers and their ballets, it is equally in its dancers. In the beginning there were very few British dancers, and they seemed to crop up wherever ballet was performed—at the Vic and the Wells, at Marie Rambert's Ballet Club, the Camargo Society, even in musical comedies, revues, cabarets, and music halls. Dancers like Alicia Markova and Anton Dolin who had been soloists with the Diaghilev ballet were glad to give the young company the benefit ·of their experience, especially when opportunities to dance in ballets like *Swan Lake* and *Giselle* were not that frequent; for Markova the collaboration with Ashton at a formative stage of her career (she had been in her teens when with Diaghilev) was of crucial importance in her growth as an artist.

But the time came when Markova felt the need to dance before a wider audience and it became necessary for de Valois to find a ballerina within her own company: as we know the choice fell on Margot Fonteyn, who had been, like Markova, a pupil of Astafieva. Fonteyn was carefully groomed for this position, assuming one by one the ballerina rôles in classical and modern ballets. By a happy coincidence, this process began at the same time as Ashton's permanent association with the company. Fonteyn became his ideal interpreter—nearly all his important ballets from *Le Baiser de la fée* in 1936 through *Ondine* in 1958 were created with her in mind, and there was one more after that, *Marguerite and Armand* (1963), in which he paid ultimate homage both to Fonteyn and to the ballerina who had first awakened in him the determination to pursue a career in ballet—Anna Pavlova.

Whole generations of dancers have grown up, passed into maturity— and some into retirement—while Fonteyn has continued to reign as undisputed prima ballerina assoluta of the company, of the world. A new standard of virtuosity was set by Nadia Nerina, first in her variation in *Birthday Offering*, then in *La Fille mal gardée* (1960); at about the same time Svetlana Beriosova, Anya Linden, and Lynn Seymour were coming to the fore, closely followed by Antoinette Sibley and Merle Park, Monica Mason, Georgina Parkinson, and Deanne Bergsma, Ann Jenner and Jennifer Penney, and more recently Lesley Collier and Laura Connor.

Although all the dancers named are listed alphabetically among the Principal category, there is no doubt that Sibley and Park are at the moment first among equals.

Merle Park seems to be Nureyev's preferred partner now that Fonteyn no longer dances the full-length ballets—a dancer of rare musicality and a delicious sense of comedy, in whom Ashton discovered, as only he can, hidden depths of passion when he choreographed *The Walk to the Paradise Garden* for her.

Antoinette Sibley is capable of scintillating virtuosity and elegance in *Scènes de ballet, La Bayadère*, or Balanchine's *Piano Concerto No. 2* (formerly *Ballet Imperial*), but she is perhaps most deeply involved when portraying wild, half-human creatures like Odette/Odile, Titania in *The Dream*— even her Manon is most striking in the problematical third act, when she takes amazing risks, both technically and dramatically, and makes it all work through her febrile intensity; no dancer can efface the memory of Fonteyn as Chloë, but Sibley has given the role her own kind of vulnerability—if *Ondine* could be revived, it should be for her.

Svetlana Beriosova seems sadly now to be relinquishing most of her ballerina rôles, but it is to be hoped that she will at least continue to invest the Bride in *Les Noces* and the Lady in *Enigma Variations* with her grave, elegiac dignity.

Lynn Seymour has assumed the position of guest artist, and while *Anastasia*, *Dances at a Gathering* and the spirited heroine of *The Two Pigeons* will continue to benefit from her rare artistry, that will not entirely compensate for the loss of her deeply moving portrayal of the girl in *The Invitation*; though never a virtuoso ballerina, Seymour has a sense of style and a kind of commitment that made her an unforgettable Giselle.

Monica Mason is a dancer of extraordinary gifts—technically amazingly strong, an actress at once powerful and sensitive, equally at home in classic rôles like Odette/Odile and in contemporary ballets like *Song of the Earth* and *Dances at a Gathering*.

Georgina Parkinson is another dancer of strong dramatic gifts, especially notable in the MacMillan repertory—a passionate Juliet, capable too of bringing vividly to life a minor character, Rosaline, in the same ballet; very distinguished, too, was her recreation of the Girl in Blue Velvet in *Les Biches*.

Deanne Bergsma has a gentle wit and graciousness that make her the ideal Lilac Fairy, a sense of the absurd that made her a hilarious Josephine in *A Wedding Bouquet*—but she can also produce the baleful glitter and commanding presence—not to mention a beautifully liquid *pas de bourrée*—for the best Queen of the Wilis to be seen anywhere.

Ann Jenner's gaiety and swift, light jump have made her the best successor to the role of Lise in *La Fille mal gardée* so far; her debut in *Giselle* showed exceptional promise, as did a *Beauty* in New York a couple of seasons ago.

Jennifer Penney, if one may venture a prediction, will be the company's next prima ballerina—her musicality and the elegance of her line have never been in question, but oddly enough it seems to have been MacMillan's creation of *The Seven Deadly Sins* for her in 1973—which no one would claim to be a major work—that has given her a new assurance; at all events, she danced an Aurora later in the same year in which her *équilibres* were breathtaking, and more recently ravishing performances of *Scènes de ballet*.

Lesley Collier is one of those dancers who seems to open up the space around her, who can, moreover, turn an audience on by communicating to them her own joy in dancing; a mischievous Lise and a captivating heroine in *Two Pigeons*, she makes both of these roles enormously touching too.

Laura Connor, like Collier, is a dancer for whom ballerina status is assured—she has already made an auspicious beginning with authoritative performances of *Raymonda* and *La Bayadère*; in *Dances at a Gathering*, too, she danced with a swiftness and breadth of which a few years ago no one would have thought a British dancer capable.

In the old touring company dancers like Lucette Aldous, Alfreda Thorogood and Doreen Wells helped to build up a new public for ballet outside London: Aldous has gone on to conquer new territory in the Southern Hemisphere, and her performances with the Australian Ballet in London in 1973 show that she is a real star; Thorogood has happily returned to the company after a season's absence; it is a great pity that Wells has found it necessary to part company with the Royal Ballet, leaving behind memories of two very touching performances of *Two Pigeons* at the beginning of the 1974 summer season and of a dazzling account of *Piano Concerto No. 2* the year before (and these are only the most vivid and recent images of a much loved dancer). In the touring company in its present guise dancers like Margaret Barbieri, Vyvyan Lorrayne, and Marion Tait, like their predecessors, are building their own devoted following.

So far we have dealt mainly with the women of the company, but the men have shown an equally extraordinary improvement within the last fifteen years. This is often attributed to the presence of Nureyev since he became the first of the famous defectors from the Kirov in 1961, and while his importance as a model should not be underrated, it must also be remembered that the men of the company had been going from strength to strength since Michael Somes, Henry Danton, and Brian Shaw first rose to the challenge of *Symphonic Variations* in 1946. Just as *La Fille mal gardée* set a new standard of female virtuosity, David Blair in the same ballet pushed masculine technique to new limits—Nureyev's arrival only hastened the process, and it continues thanks to the friendly rivalry that subsists among the leading men.

Anthony Dowell is the equal of any male classical dancer now before the public, and has become in more recent years a wonderful dance actor as well; in this respect the experience of working with Tudor on *Shadowplay* brought about a transformation in Dowell, though Ashton's choice of him as Sibley's consort in *The Dream* a couple of years earlier had also made new interpretive demands on him as well as creating a partnership that was to become second only to that of Fonteyn and Nureyev in terms of star quality.

David Wall, like Doreen Wells, had built up his own following in his years with the touring company; he is perhaps a more natural actor than Dowell and that much less pure a classicist, a dancer who can seemingly without effort bring to life the dukes and princes of the nineteenth century ballets, and in *Manon* create a portrait of the heroine's unscrupulous brother that manages to be charming and funny as well as totally convincing.

Michael Coleman both in technique and sunny personality is the best Colas since Blair; it has been well said of him that he could be a really great dancer if he would only take himself a little more seriously—and a recent performance of Albrecht, well thought out and deeply felt, has suggested that he is beginning to do just that.

Desmond Kelly, also a wonderful and very original Albrecht, whose range also encompasses such Balanchine ballets as *Apollo*, *Agon*, and *The Prodigal Son*, must be considered a close runner-up to these three.

Donald MacLeary, like Kelly, is the favourite partner of many ballerinas, unfailingly considerate and secure; as the protagonist of MacMillan's *Song of the Earth*, opposite Dowell's sinister Messenger of Death, he gives a deeply moving performance, and shows another side of his talent in the deft footwork of *Elite Syncopations*.

As for character dancers, it is safe to say that there are no more distinguished artists anywhere than Alexander Grant, whose Alain in *Fille* is, incredibly, as nimble, funny, and touching as ever; Derek Rencher, whose character portrayals range from an outrageous Duke of Courland in *Giselle* (surely a not too distant relation of Henry VIII?) to the Elgar of *Enigma Variations*; the veteran Leslie Edwards, whether as the rubicund farmer Thomas in *Fille* or the King in *Sleeping Beauty* (it is not without any intention of demoting him that one may express a preference for his harassed but always gallant Cantalabutte); and Stanley Holden, officially retired, who still returns from time to time to delight us with his hilarious, loving Widow Simone.

Of the younger generation David Ashmole, Wayne Eagling, Graham Fletcher, Nicholas Johnson, Mark Silver and Michael Corder are much more than merely promising, while the touring company has at least two very gifted and versatile male dancers in Alain Dubreuil and Stephen Jefferies.

The Royal Ballet today is in fact a company of extraordinary strength and diversity: the roster as now printed in the programme lists no fewer than forty-five principals, of whom eight are guest artists—though of these only Makarova, Nureyev, Barishnikov and Gielgud are not previous full-time members; nineteen Solo Artists; twenty-three Coryphés; and fifty-eight Artists. Many dancers in the Solo and Coryphé categories often assume principal roles, and for that matter those described simply as "Artists" are not exclusively to be found in the *corps de ballet*. Out of this total of 145 have to be drawn the personnel not only for the main company at Covent Garden but also for the touring company and Ballet for All, with a constant interchange among these divisions. In short, there has been a quantitative no less than a qualitative transformation of the company in the twenty-eight years since it first took possession of the Royal Opera House.

As for the repertory, the nineteenth century classics are still the mainstay, though all of them have gone through several revisions since the pre-war days when the method of putting on a classic ballet was for the dancers to be taught the choreography by Nicholas Sergeyev, former *régisseur* of the Maryinsky Theatre in St Petersburg, from his notebooks containing the old Stepanov notation. There was very little then in the way of production or "interpretation," and even now the Royal Ballet versions preserve what may be called the irreducible minimum of the original choreography, avoiding some of the more extravagant "improvements" to be found elsewhere.

Thus, *The Sleeping Beauty* has seen two completely new versions in the last six years, neither of them, in the opinion of many, preferable to the old 1946 version that held the stage for more than twenty years. *Swan Lake*, after being given for a while in a rather more eccentric version than is usual with the Royal Ballet, has reverted to the Petipa-Ivanov original in as authentic a state as we are likely to see, retaining a few of Ashton's additions, notably the Neapolitan Dance that has stopped the show ever since it was first given by Julia Farron and Alexander Grant in 1952, and the brilliant classic *pas de quatre*. One may regret the loss of his arrangement of the fourth act, a kind of homage to Ivanov

and a beautiful elegiac choreographic poem in its own right; one would like to see the company take up the suggestion that this be preserved as a separate item, perhaps in the touring repertory.

Another loss is the *Giselle* that Ashton lovingly recreated with the help of Tamara Karsavina. But the production has been the vehicle for notable assumptions of the title rôle by Sibley, Park, Natalia Makarova, and, in the touring company, Margaret Barbieri—each of them bringing the character to life in terms that have contemporary validity as well as remaining true to the Romantic style of the piece. Dowell, Wall, Kelly, and Coleman have all given distinguished performances of Albrecht.

The Nutcracker is an indispensable item in any repertory nowadays: Sergeyev's reconstruction of the original Ivanov has long been lost, and so alas! is the short version Ashton made for the old second company. The current Royal Ballet production is the work of Rudolf Nureyev and is the most interesting of recent attempts to make sense of the story in adult terms. No one has improved on Ivanov's choreography for the *pas de deux* (and Ashton did not try to), but Nureyev has made some beautiful dances for the *corps de ballet* and an exquisite pastoral *pas de trois*; throughout, there are pleasing touches of humour.

Nureyev's memory for the ballets he danced in Soviet Russia is as prodigious as any other aspect of his talent, and his productions of single acts from two Petipa masterpieces, *Raymonda* and *La Bayadère*, are among his most important contributions to the Royal Ballet. Without first-hand knowledge it would be impossible to comment on the authenticity of their detail, but they seem to be true to the spirit of the originals—and certainly provide the dancers with opportunities to show the brilliance and authority of their classical style. *Bayadère* especially seems to be the work that has brought the Royal *corps de ballet* to its present level, surely unequalled in the world today. There can be no greater thrill for the balletomane than to see these dancers make their entrance—that astoundingly audacious piece of choreography a seemingly endless file coming down the ramp in *penchée arabesques* repeated ad infinitum—especially in New York in the spring of 1974, when night after night they seemed to be tuned to an ever higher pitch of perfection. And that is only the beginning, for what a company it is that can put on to the stage not only such a *corps* but soloists like Bergsma, Collier, Connor, Jenner, Mason, Penney, to say nothing of Ria Peri and Marguerite Porter, in the subsidiary variations, *danseurs* like Dowell, Wall, and Coleman who all give Nureyev a run for his money in the role of Solor, ballerinas of the calibre of Sibley and Park! At such times there can be no doubt in one's mind that one is watching the greatest company in the world.

Kenneth MacMillan, as director, must be given credit for this continuing improvement in the standard of dancing. Since returning to Covent Garden in that capacity he has made two new full-length ballets, *Anastasia* and *Manon*, that have tried to enlarge the possibilities of the kind of subject-matter that this form of ballet can deal with. He has also contributed several shorter, slighter works like *Triad*, *The Seven Deadly Sins*, and *Elite Syncopations*.

De Valois is now hardly represented in the repertory of the main company, except for occasional revivals of *Job* and, less frequently, *Checkmate* (*The Rake's Progress* happily remains a standard of the touring repertory), but many of the great Ashton ballets remain, under the jealous custody of Michael Somes: *Symphonic Variations*, *Scènes de ballet*, and *Monotones*—statements of his credo as a choreographer; the two hilarious and tender longer ballets, *La Fille mal gardée* and *The Two Pigeons*; and one-act works like *Daphnis and Chloë*, *Enigma Variations*, and *The Dream* that show the extraordinary range of expression that classic ballet is capable of. Since his retirement Ashton has made a few miniatures of which one, *Thaïs*, for Sibley and Dowell, is a masterpiece, and his admirers, both among the dancers and the public, do not cease to hope that he will come out of retirement before long to give them another major work. At Ashton's age, after all, Petipa had still to create two of his greatest masterpieces, *The Sleeping Beauty* and *Raymonda*.

Which brings us to the question of the future of the Royal Ballet, and since that is of course unpredictable the writer may be forgiven for continuing in this vein of wishful thinking. First, the company needs a theatre of its own that it does not have to share with the Royal Opera. As I have already indicated, there is undeniably an extra excitement in their performances in New York that comes partly from an audience response that is not jaded through familiarity, partly from the fact that the company is keyed up from giving eight performances a week instead of only three or four. For the performing artist of whatever kind there is simply no substitute for regular and frequent exercise of his or her talents in front of an audience. Moreover with a company the size of the Royal Ballet opportunities to per-form important roles come round too seldom for the dancers to grow in them.

Second, one would like to see the dancers challenged still further by new choreography of a contemporary kind. There is presumably no danger of the Royal Ballet neglecting its responsibilities towards the classic repertory, but a ballet company cannot function only as a museum. Without doubt the experience of working on Robbins's *Dances at a Gathering* was the occasion of a breakthrough for several members of that cast, and Monica Mason's performance in Macmillan's *Rite of Spring* and David Wall's in Tetley's *Laborintus* showed that they are not only great classical dancers but great modern dancers too. True, a start has been made with the commissions from Tetley, van Dantzig and van Manen, even if no ballet in the repertory seems more modern than Nijinska's *Les Noces*, that staggering masterpiece, but the directors could be still more adventurous in this area. Merce Cunningham and Twyla Tharp are only two contemporary choreographers who have already shown that they can use dancers in a traditional ballet company in ways that stretch their powers without (and this is important) negating the technical equipment their training has given them.

Third, and absolutely essential if the dancers are to take the next giant step forward, the company must strive to develop in its dancers a greater musicality and sense of rhythm, and in its musical staff a greater awareness of dancers' needs, as opposed to their whims. This is the more serious because the dancers are at a point where they need to add a greater speed and sharpness of attack to their already impressive technical equipment—and they can do it, they can do anything if they are given a chance, because they are among the most marvellous dancers in the world.

3. *Swan Lake. Corps de ballet*

4. *Swan Lake* rehearsal. Doreen Wells and David Wall

5. *Swan Lake*. Antoinette Sibley and Anthony Dowell

6

7

6. *Swan Lake*. Svetlana Beriosova and Donald MacLeary
7. *Swan Lake*. Lesley Collier and David Ashmole

8. *Swan Lake*. Antoinette Sibley and Anthony Dowell

9. *Swan Lake*. Doreen Wells and David Wall

10

11

10. *Swan Lake*. Anthony Dowell
11. *Swan Lake*. Antoinette Sibley and Anthony Dowell

12. *The Firebird*. Antoinette Sibley
14. *Les Biches*. Jennifer Penney and Ann Jenner

13. *The Firebird*. Merle Park and David Wall
15. *The Prodigal Son*. Rudolf Nureyev

16. *Le Corsaire*. Margot Fonteyn and Rudolf Nureyev

17

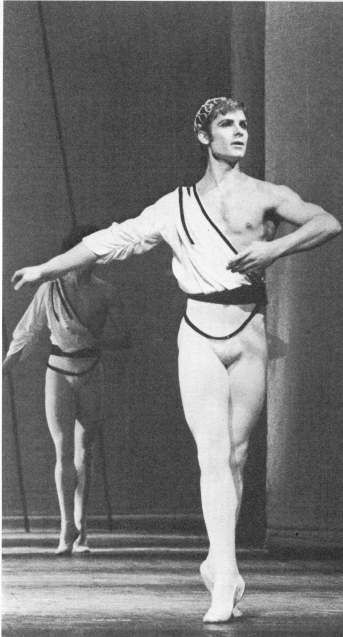

18

17. *Symphonic Variations*. Antoinette Sibley
18. *Symphonic Variations*. David Wall

19. *Symphonic Variations*. Jennifer Penney, Michael Coleman and Gary Sherwood

20

21

20 and 21. *Symphonic Variations*. Merle Park and David Wall

22. *Romeo and Juliet*. Anthony Dowell

23. *Romeo and Juliet.* Lesley Collier and Gerd Larsen

24. *Romeo and Juliet*. Lynn Seymour and David Wall

25. *Romeo and Juliet*. Georgina Parkinson

26. *Romeo and Juliet*. Antoinette Sibley and Anthony Dowell

27. *Romeo and Juliet*. David Wall
29. *Romeo and Juliet*. Desmond Doyle

28. *Romeo and Juliet*. Wayne Eagling
30. *Romeo and Juliet*. David Wall and Michael Coleman

31

32

31. *Romeo and Juliet*. Merle Park
32. *Romeo and Juliet*. Lynn Seymour and David Wall

33. *Dances at a Gathering*. Antoinette Sibley, Lynn Seymour and Laura Connor
34. *Dances at a Gathering*. Rudolf Nureyev, Anthony Dowell and David Wall

35. *Dances at a Gathering*. Monica Mason and Michael Coleman
36. *Dances at a Gathering*. Laura Connor, Ann Jenner, David Wall, Rudolf Nureyev and Anthony Dowell

37

38

39

37. *Dances at a Gathering*. Antoinette Sibley and Anthony Dowell
38. *Dances at a Gathering*. Monica Mason
39. *Dances at a Gathering*. Antoinette Sibley and Michael Coleman

40. *Dances at a Gathering*. Ann Jenner and Anthony Dowell

41

42

43

41. *Apollo*. Svetlana Beriosova
42. *Apollo*. Monica Mason and Georgina Parkinson
43. *Apollo*. Svetlana Beriosova, Rudolf Nureyev and Vergie Derman

44. *Apollo*. Desmond Kelly

45

46

45. *Daphnis and Chloë*. Georgina Parkinson and Anthony Dowell
46. *Daphnis and Chloë*. Antoinette Sibley and Anthony Dowell

47

48

47. *Daphnis and Chloë*. Anthony Dowell
48. *Daphnis and Chloë*. Merle Park and Alexander Grant

49

50

49. *The Nutcracker*. Carole Hill, Wayne Sleep and Lesley Collier
50. *The Nutcracker*. Antoinette Sibley and Anthony Dowell

51. *The Nutcracker*. Merle Park

52. *Pavane*. Antoinette Sibley and Anthony Dowell

53

54

53. *La Bayadère*. Anthony Dowell
54. *La Bayadère*. Laura Connor

55

56

55. *La Bayadère. Corps de ballet*
56. *Les Sylphides*. Natalia Makarova and Anthony Dowell

57. *Les Sylphides*. Natalia Makarova, Anthony Dowell and Lesley Collier

58. *A Wedding Bouquet*. Jennifer Penney and Alexander Grant

59

60

59. *A Wedding Bouquet*. Deanne Bergsma
60. *A Wedding Bouquet*. Robert Helpmann

61

62

63

61. *Anastasia*. Lynn Seymour
62. *Anastasia*. Derek Rencher, Lynn Seymour and Svetlana Beriosova
63. *Anastasia*. Svetlana Beriosova and Lynn Seymour

64. *Anastasia*. Lynn Seymour and David Adams

65

66

67

65 and 66. *Shadowplay*. Anthony Dowell
67. *In the Night*. Antoinette Sibley

68. *In the Night*. Antoinette Sibley and Anthony Dowell

69. *The Walk to the Paradise Garden.* Merle Park and David Wall

70

71

72

70. *The Seven Deadly Sins.* Georgia Brown and Jennifer Penney
71. *Elite Syncopations.* Jennifer Penney and David Wall
72. *Four Schumann Pieces.* Jennifer Penney and Anthony Dowell

73. *Giselle*. Antoinette Sibley and Anthony Dowell

74

75

74. *Giselle*. David Wall
75. *Giselle*. Antoinette Sibley

76

77

78

76. *Giselle* rehearsal. Natalia Makarova and Anthony Dowell
77. *Giselle*. Ann Jenner
78. *Giselle*. Doreen Wells and David Wall

79. *Giselle*. Ann Jenner

80. *Giselle*. Merle Park and Anthony Dowell

81

82

81. *Giselle*. Antoinette Sibley
82. *Giselle*. Ann Jenner and Desmond Kelly

83. *Jazz Calendar*. Anthony Dowell, Merle Park and Robert Mead
84. *Jazz Calendar*. Antoinette Sibley and Rudolf Nureyev

85. *Les Noces*. Svetlana Beriosova

86. *Afternoon of a Faun*. Jennifer Penney

87. *Afternoon of a Faun*. Anthony Dowell
88. *Afternoon of a Faun*. Antoinette Sibley and Anthony Dowell
89. *Afternoon of a Faun*. Jennifer Penney and Rudolf Nureyev

90. *The Two Pigeons*. Doreen Wells

91

92

91. *The Two Pigeons*. David Wall
92. *The Two Pigeons*. Ann Jenner

93

94

93. *The Two Pigeons*. Doreen Wells and David Wall
94. *The Two Pigeons*. Lynn Seymour and David Wall

95. *Requiem Canticles*. Wayne Eagling

96

97

96. *The Dream*. Lucette Aldous
97. *Serenade*. Laura Connor

98. *Cinderella*. Margot Fonteyn

99

100

101

99. *Cinderella*. Ria Peri
100. *Cinderella*. Antoinette Sibley
101. *Cinderella*. Wayne Sleep, Robert Helpmann and Frederick Ashton

102. *Cinderella*. Antoinette Sibley and Anthony Dowell

103

104

103. *Cinderella*. Margot Fonteyn
104. *Cinderella*. Robert Helpmann and Frederick Ashton

105

106

107

105. *Scènes de ballet*. Antoinette Sibley
106. *Birthday Offering*. Merle Park and Donald MacLeary
107. Meditation from *Thaïs*. Antoinette Sibley and Anthony Dowell

108. *Concerto*. Natalia Makarova and Donald MacLeary

109

110

109. *Concerto*. Jennifer Penney
110. *Concerto*. Monica Mason

111

112

111. *La Fille mal gardée*. Anthony Dowell
112. *La Fille mal gardée*. Alexander Grant

113. *La Fille mal gardée*. Michael Coleman

114. *La Fille mal gardée*. Rudolf Nureyev

115. *Triad*. Anthony Dowell

116

117

118

116. *Triad*. Wayne Eagling, Antoinette Sibley and Anthony Dowell
117. *Triad*. Wayne Eagling and Anthony Dowell
118. *Agon*. Laura Connor

119. *Les Rendezvous*. Merle Park

120

121

120. *Manon.* Anthony Dowell
121. *Manon.* David Wall

122. *Manon*. Antoinette Sibley and Anthony Dowell

123

124

125

123. *Manon*. Antoinette Sibley and David Wall
124. *Manon*. Antoinette Sibley
125. *Manon*. Antoinette Sibley and Anthony Dowell

126. *Manon*. Anthony Dowell

127

128

127. *Manon*. Laura Connor and Vergie Derman
128. *Manon*. Derek Rencher and Antoinette Sibley

129. *Manon*. Antoinette Sibley and Anthony Dowell
130. *Manon*. David Wall
131. *Manon*. Gerd Larsen and Julian Hosking

132. *Enigma Variations*. Anthony Dowell

133

134

133. *Enigma Variations*. Desmond Doyle, Anthony Dowell, Derek Rencher and Svetlana Beriosova
134. *Enigma Variations*. Svetlana Beriosova and Derek Rencher

135. *Enigma Variations*. Deanne Bergsma

136

137

138

136. *Enigma Variations*. Brian Shaw
137. *Lilac Garden*. Antoinette Sibley and Anthony Dowell
138. *The Ropes of Time*. Diana Vere, Rudolf Nureyev and Monica Mason

139

140

139. *Song of the Earth*. Anthony Dowell and Donald MacLeary
140. *Song of the Earth*. Monica Mason and Donald MacLeary

141

142

143

141. *Song of the Earth*. Kenneth Mason and Anthony Dowell
142. *Song of the Earth*. Monica Mason and Anthony Dowell
143. *Song of the Earth*. Anthony Dowell, Monica Mason and Donald MacLeary

144. *Song of the Earth*. Anthony Dowell

145. *The Sleeping Beauty*. David Drew, Keith Rosson, Antoinette Sibley and Derek Rencher

146. *The Sleeping Beauty.* Antoinette Sibley

147

148

147. *The Sleeping Beauty*. Antoinette Sibley and Donald MacLeary
148. *The Sleeping Beauty*. Antoinette Sibley and Anthony Dowell

149. *The Sleeping Beauty*. Alfreda Thorogood and Michael Coleman

150. *The Sleeping Beauty*. Wayne Sleep
152. *The Sleeping Beauty*. Antoinette Sibley

151. *The Sleeping Beauty*. Anthony Dowell
153. *The Sleeping Beauty*. Laura Connor

154. *The Sleeping Beauty*. Margot Fonteyn taking a curtain call